Who Lies There?

The lives of some of those buried in the churchyard of St Nicholas Chislehurst

GW00724814

Compiled by
The Chislehurst Society Evening History Group

Jenny Allen, Don Drage, Alan and Catherine Fyfield, Joanna Friel,
Lesley Reed, Pat Waters and Una White.

OCBC
Old Chapel Books, Chislehurst

Published in Great Britain by
Old Chapel Books, Chislehurst,
The Old Chapel, Queens Passage, Chislehurst, BR7 5AP

First published
June 2018

Paperback ISBN 978-1-912236-10-7

Printed in Great Britain by
Copy & Print Ltd
www.copyandprint.co

*Cover photo: thank you to Tony Breen of Eagle Drones for his permission
to use the aerial photograph of St Nicholas Church.
http://www.eagledrones.london*

Contents

The locations of the graves mentioned here are indicated on the map of the churchyard reproduced on the back cover.

Introduction

How little room
Do we take up in death that living, know
No bounds?

James Shirley 1596-1666

The subjects of this booklet are a disparate collection of people. Members of the History Group were given a free hand in their research, the only criterion being that their subject should have an identifiable grave in the churchyard. Their approaches to the task were various: some started with a character and then sought out their burial plot; others were attracted to an unusual gravestone; yet others used the Kent Archaeological Society Monumental Inscriptions site to locate interesting inscriptions.

It was only when all the articles were brought together, that it became clear we had assembled a cross-section of Chislehurst society spanning the 18th to 20th centuries. There are figures here of national and international renown as well as those whose names were known only in the locality, but all lives have something to tell.

It was also interesting to discover the interconnectedness of many of the subjects. Some had lived in the same house at different periods; George Miller had designed Willett's memorial; Jessie Drummond had cared for the boys at the Orphanage and Anne Taylor taught them; George Merry was Alexander Gamble's nephew and there are other links to be found.

These people lived in very class-conscious times but in death there is no distinction. The landed gentry lie with those of humble birth.

Pat Waters
Editor
June 2018

1. William Willett

This grave is located in the south-east corner of the churchyard.

William Willett jnr. was born in 1856 in Farnham, Surrey. He and his father were builders of some repute having developed estates in London and Dover. Willett came to Chislehurst in 1894 and lived in his newly-built house, The Cedars, at the top of Old Hill opposite the gates to Camden Place. He had purchased the Camden Place estate in 1890 with the intention of developing it with three hundred homes. However, this plan failed after a legal battle over rights of way across Chislehurst Common. Camden Place Golf Club was developed instead.

As a riding enthusiast Willett enjoyed the Commons and rode his horse early in the morning through the woods, making the most of the daylight hours. Daylight was to be his crusade. His houses were typified by large windows allowing sunlight to pour in and his increasingly tenacious campaign to change the clocks became as hotly debated as votes for women.

Between 1907 and 1914 he wrote and distributed fifteen pamphlets on what he termed 'Wasting the Daylight'. He championed the cause, stating it would improve the health and happiness of everyone as well as save the country £2.5 million on electricity (£300m today). Funds for his campaign came from his house-building and his supporters included Arthur Conan Doyle, King Edward VII, Lloyd George and Churchill. But his complicated methodology for saving the daylight, which involved changing the clocks by twenty minutes across four weeks, failed to win approval in Parliament.

Willett was a philanthropic man, a supporter of Bromley Cottage Hospital and involved himself in Red Cross work to convert local houses into hospitals for the wounded from the Western Front. He was head of the Chislehurst Masonic Lodge, which met at Camden Place and there was even a waxwork of him at Madame Tussauds.

Willett died in March 1915, aged only 58, never knowing that his idea would come to fruition. His early death is said to have prevented his knighthood as a social reformer.

William Willett and his daughter Gertrude

2. The de Quincey Quincey family

The grave, on which stands a decorated stone cross, is to the right of the path from the lychgate to the church.

The memorial records the deaths of Roger de Quincey Quincey, his wife Elizabeth, their sons Richard and Edmund together with an inscription to their grandson Thomas, who is listed as 'wounded and missing in France May 9th 1915.

Roger came to live at Oakwood House, Yester Road, (no longer in existence) in 1896, when he was around 69 years old. After the death of his wife Elizabeth in the same year, he continued to live at Oakwood House with two of his daughters: Mary aged 40 and Marian 33. Roger's occupation is listed in the 1901 census as 'retired East India merchant'. He was obviously a very wealthy man as he was able to employ sixteen servants. His home is described by Arthur Battle in his book *Edwardian Chislehurst* as being 'a proud Victorian mansion with a lake and boathouse'.

Battle also mentions that the family was renowned for the successful breeding and showing of Sealyham terriers. Roger died in 1906.

His son Richard, a foreign and colonial merchant resided at Inglewood House (now part of Bullerswood School) with his wife Ruth and five children. Richard died at Inglewood in 1924.

Thomas de Quincey Quincey, Richard's eldest son was 20 years old in 1914 and joined the 2nd Battalion Rifle Brigade, holding the rank of second lieutenant. He received the 1914-1915 Star. However, whilst serving in France Thomas was listed wounded and missing in action; his body was never found. In a probate record of 1920 his date of death was given as the 9th May 1915, a date which coincides with the Battle of Aubers Ridge His name is commemorated on the Ploegsteert Memorial in Belgium, which commemorates more than 11,000 servicemen of the United Kingdom and South African forces who died in this sector and have no known graves.

As he was recorded as 'missing' Thomas's name was not originally recorded on the Chislehurst War Memorial. His name was added to the list of fallen in November 2015.

The last name on the family memorial is Edmund de Quincey Quincey, Roger and Elizabeth's eldest son, a merchant, who lived at Oakwood House. He died in 1929.

The evolution of the surname 'de Quincey Quincey' has an interesting history. It was first introduced into England by followers of William the Conqueror in 1066. Originally Roger's father who came from Lincolnshire was just plain Richard Quincey. He moved to London where he did well in business and adopted the name of de Quincey, possibly inspired by his distant cousin Thomas de Quincey, who wrote the book *Confessions of an English Opium Eater*. Roger, wishing to distinguish his own branch of the family called himself de Quincey Quincey. He must have felt even more distinguished when, in 1895, he received an invitation to attend the funeral of his cousin, the dress designer Charles Worth, addressed to 'Monsieur et Madame Roger de Quincé-Quincey'.

Roger de Quincey Quincey

*Elizabeth de Quincey Quincey, wife
of Roger*

*Edmund de Quincey Quincey, son of
Roger and Elizabeth*

3. Sir George Hayter Chubb

The grave is located near the fence to the right of the path from the lychgate to the church.

George Hayter Chubb (1848-1946) was the grandson of Charles Chubb, founder of the famous firm Chubb & Sons Lock and Safe Co. From 1882 until his death he was Managing Director and for a time Chairman of the internationally renowned company. It supplied security devices for the Post Office, prisons, museums and hotels. The 1914 catalogue lists 314 safes, 18 strong rooms and numerous locks.

In 1870 George married Sarah Vanner Early, a member of a prominent Chislehurst Methodist family. The couple moved into Newlands, a house on the site of what is now Maxwell House in Prince Imperial Road next to the Methodist Church, which Sarah's family had been instrumental in building. George's mother moved into a house next door to her son called Chevender, which means chubb fish. Regular worshippers at the Methodist Church, the family is remembered by a plaque on the wall near the pew they regularly occupied. There is a memorial window to Sir George's father, John Chubb (1815- 1872) on the north wall. Sir George, Lord Hayter, was artistic and a great craftsman; he taught himself woodcarving and made the beautiful lectern still in use in the church today.

Although the firm was the centre of his concerns, his interests and involvements were vast. He was a great philanthropist, churchman, educationalist as well as a business man. He supported the Duchess of Albany's Deptford Fund (after whom Albany Road is named), which resulted in what is now the Albany Community Centre, the Royal Navy Fund and many more charities.

Most significantly he was a Governor of the Leys Methodist School for boys in Cambridge and was the first Chair of the Governors of Farringtons School in Chislehurst, its counterpart for girls (though today it is a co-educational establishment). He was responsible for the visits of Queen Mary to the school (see photograph below). In 1934 Lady Hayter formally unlocked the great bronze doors of the newly-built school chapel. The doors had been cast by Chubb and Co. in Sydney, Australia.

Knighted by Queen Victoria in 1885, made a baronet in 1900, George was created 1st Baron Hayter (his mother's maiden name) of Chiselhurst (his spelling) in 1927. He was Justice of the Peace for Kent and the oldest member of the House of Lords when he died at Newlands on 7th November 1946, two years before his 100th birthday.

He is buried alongside his wife and daughter who pre-deceased him. His legacy as a local benefactor remains strong (just like his safes) in the village and even the Farringtons School badge contains a key as one of its elements.

4. Richard Foster

The flat gravestone is located in the area to the right of the lychgate as you enter.

In 1881 a gentleman who signed himself simply 'a London merchant' in a letter to the Rector of Rotherhithe, told him that in 'daily journeys by train from his home in Chislehurst he had noted the rapid growth of humble streets overtopped only by large public houses and board schools and that his heart was moved with the desire to plant a church of brick and mortar in this barren wilderness which was rapidly swallowing up the country fields'.

The London merchant was Mr Richard Foster, a foreign trader, who lived on the large Homewood estate in Perry Street. He was a keen horseman, originally from Clapton, but when that area became over-developed he moved to the more rural south London suburb. He offered a sum of £2,000 to Bishop Thorold of Rochester, and so began the Bishop's Ten Churches Fund, a scheme to renovate or build ten new churches in impoverished areas.

A site was obtained in Eugenia Road, Rotherhithe for the new church of St Katharine and the Rev. Francis Murray of St Nicholas, Chislehurst, laid the foundation stone. Foster along with Canon Murray took up the notion of 'associated parishes', in which a richer parish took a special interest in the welfare of a particularly poor parish. For a brief period the Chislehurst parish magazine was officially titled *Chislehurst and St Katharine, Rotherhithe Parish Magazine*. The link between Chislehurst and Rotherhithe gave Foster a good deal of work to the end of his life, which came in 1910 when he was 88. He left an estate worth over £188,000

Richard Foster's gravestone

Homewood, Foster's home

5. The Firbank Family

This triple grave with ornate carvings lies to the right of the lychgate as you approach the church.

Thomas Firbank inherited his fortune from his father, Joseph, a self-educated coal miner-cum-engineer, who had made his money in the nineteenth century by investing in the conversion of Welsh canals into railways. Thomas himself was a railway contractor. He married the wealthy Lady Harriette Garrett, a minor Irish aristocrat and socialite and they came to live at The Coopers, now Coopers School Sixth Form Centre in Hawkwood Lane, where they employed a staff of seventeen. Thomas was MP for Hull and knighted in 1901. His two youngest children, Hubert and Heather, were born in Chislehurst in 1887 and 1888 respectively.

Tragedy struck in 1904 when the eldest son, Joey, died of a mysterious illness. His was the first body to be buried in the family plot. Sir Thomas died in 1910 and was buried alongside his son. Hubert died in Canada in 1913 and he too is interred here, as is Lady Harriette, who passed away in 1924.

But it is the legacy of the remaining two children which is most notable.

(Arthur Annesley) Ronald Firbank, (pictured below), born in 1886, became an avant-garde author, much influenced by Oscar Wilde and the Aesthetic Movement. His first novel, *Odette d'Antrevernes*, published at his own expense in 1905 when he was nineteen, is a slight, sentimental piece full of over-blown descriptions of fragrant flowers and twittering birds, perhaps based on the beautiful gardens of The Coopers, but later works such as *Vainglory*, *Valmouth* and *Flower Beneath the Foot* display wit and precision, much admired by Evelyn Waugh. The now unacceptably titled *Prancing Nigger* is a tale of racial discrimination, social climbing and religion.

Ronald died in 1926 in Rome of pneumonia. His sister had his body exhumed from the Protestant graveyard, where he had been buried mistakenly. He was a Catholic, who had converted to the faith when he was an undergraduate at Cambridge and was received into the Church by Monsignor Robert Hugh Benson. He was reinterred in a Catholic plot but still in Rome. The Coopers stands opposite the celebrated little church of St Mary, which at the end of the 19th century was a centre of the Catholic revival. It was founded in 1854 by another Catholic convert, Henry Bowden, who coincidently had lived at Coopers until 1864.

Ronald's sister, Heather Firbank, had a penchant for haute couture and spent far too much of the family fortune (which was in rapid decline after 1907) at the fashion houses of Mayfair. Her brother wrote to her: "Your annuity should go towards 'Jones' the greengrocer as well as 'Lucille' the dressmaker – it seems a little stupid to have to point that out!" This is a case of the pot calling the kettle black, as Ronald lived off his inheritance, not his writing, which was largely ignored in his life-time, and spent much of his time travelling in Spain, Italy, the Middle East and north Africa indulging in a generally decadent life-style

Heather never married and in fact embarked on a disastrous affair with a married man, which only ended in bitterness and ill health, perhaps not helped by the influence of alcohol After Ronald's death, she packed away her beautiful wardrobe of fine garments, including hats and lingerie, and proceeded to lead an itinerant life, finally passing away in a nursing-home in Haywards Heath in 1954 aged 67. Her ashes were scattered in Brighton as there was no one left to make the connection to the family plot back in Chislehurst.

Her exquisite clothing collection, much of it heather-coloured to complement her name, was auctioned at Christies. Over 200 items were acquired by the V&A Museum, where they have been used as the basis of several exhibitions, notably *A London Society Wardrobe* in 1960. The Heather Firbank archive has been an inspiration for many costume designers, particularly for the team working on the outfits of Cora and Lady Mary in the television costume drama *Downton Abbey*.

The V&A has produced a lavishly illustrated book, *London Society Fashion 1905 – 1925: The Wardrobe of Heather Firbank*, by Cassie Davies-Strodder and J. Lister. The book tells Heather's full story and contains some wonderful old images of Coopers, with not a blue blazer in sight.

Heather Firbank

12

6. Malcolm Campbell

The grave is on the left of the lychgate as you face the church.

Campbell was born at Rossmore (now West Witheridge) on Prince Imperial Road on 11th March 1885, the only son of diamond merchant William Campbell. He was christened at St Nicholas Church. He was brought up with horses and could ride from the age of three. He was educated at Hornbrook House Preparatory School and appeared as a little oyster in *Alice in Wonderland* at Chislehurst Village Hall. When he was twelve Malcolm was fined thirty shillings for riding a bicycle at an estimated speed of 27mph much to the confusion and terror of two elderly ladies on Summer Hill. The magistrate said, 'I never want to see you going at such a speed again'.

The family moved to Northwood on Manor Park Road in 1894 but Malcolm left home at the age of 18 as a direct result of a heated argument with his father. He left the area only returning as a visitor. As a pilot during the First World War Malcolm used the West Kent Cricket Club ground as a landing strip when he visited his parents, who were by then at Bonchester, Camden Park Road. He was awarded an MBE in 1918 for services to flying and was knighted in February 1931.

He had a lifelong career testing himself to see how fast he could go in ever-changing models of his cars and boats, all called Bluebird. Maeterlink's 1912 operatic fantasy *The Blue Bird* about the pursuit of happiness so tantalisingly close, came to symbolise Campbell's determination to reach ever faster speeds. He achieved the land speed record in September 1935 by travelling at 301.337mph on Bonneville Flats, Utah, USA. The water speed record was achieved in August 1939 with a speed of 141.7mph on Coniston Water in the Lake District.

One of the few racing drivers to die of natural causes, Campbell – The Speed King – passed away at three minutes to midnight on New Year's Eve 1948. He died in Reigate but the funeral was held at St Nicholas Church, where he is buried with his parents. There are some in the village who can remember singing in the choir at the funeral and seeing the Bluebird motif on the coffin.

The Bluebird motif at The Ruskin Museum Coniston

7. George William Merry and George William Miller

The grave with a Celtic cross, decorated on both sides, and inscribed on the surround, is located to the left of the path from the lychgate to the church.

This is a most unusual grave in that it contains the remains of two unrelated bachelor friends, who died within a few years of each other in the 1930s

George Merry came from a family of saddlers in Leamington Spa and he worked in the business until he was 40 when for some unknown reason he moved to Chislehurst, first to Church Row and then to The White House, just to the west of the church beyond the Cockpit. The fact that

his uncle, Alexander Gamble, Master of the Horse to Napoleon III, had spent his last years in the village, may be significant. How George supported himself is also a mystery, as although on census returns he described himself as a saddler, there is no evidence of his working in the trade here. However, we do know that by 1891 he had taken in a lodger, an Irish architect, sculptor, artist and photographer 16 years his junior, called George Miller.

The two men were to live together for nigh on 50 years, becoming very supportive members of the local community. Miller was one of the three authors of Webb's *History of Chislehurst*, a scholarly work published in 1899. He also designed the memorial sundial in Petts Wood (see below) erected by local residents to honour William Willett, who had the idea of introducing National Daylight Saving Time.

On his death in 1932 George William Merry left George William Miller The White House and half his considerable fortune. Miller died in 1939, shortly after the outbreak of World War II and The White House was requisitioned by the army.

8. Thomas Brammall Daniel

The grave is immediately to the left when entering by the lychgate. It is surmounted by a praying angel.

Thomas Brammall Daniel (1873-1956) was an architect, originally from Manchester, who lived on Royal Parade. He practised in London and also in Canada, where his most notable achievement was the design for St John's Cathedral in Saskatoon.

He was also a past Master of the Worshipful Company of Glovers. This City livery company, now mainly a charitable body, maintains its original links to the glove trade by presenting the Sovereign with a special glove, which is worn at the coronation ceremony. The glove is a beautifully embroidered gauntlet, which is kept in a special box. In 1953 Brammall Daniel was the chair of a small sub-committee set up to commission the box for Elizabeth II's coronation glove. He suggested John Easden, his neighbour on Royal Parade, who had a cabinet-making business.

Two boxes, designed by Mr Daniel and made by Mr Easden, were made to fit inside each other for protection and security (see below). Once completed they were displayed for two weeks so that the people of Chislehurst could admire the craftsmanship and enjoy the honour bestowed upon two of the villagers.

9. The Stone Family

This large altar tomb is to the left of the path leading from the lychgate to the south porch. Much of the inscription is now illegible.

The large tomb memorialises some members of three generations of the family of Richard Stone (1757-1802) of Coopers, the mansion he purchased in 1784, which is now the Sixth Form Centre of Coopers School in Hawkwood Lane. Richard married Mary Herring, cousin of the Archbishop of Canterbury and his co-heir. Like his father and grandfather before him, in 1760 Richard joined the Grasshopper Bank at 68 Lombard Street, where James Martin was Senior Partner in the long-established banking house. For the next ninety years the bank's business was conducted mainly by these two families. Their business connections were further cemented by the marriage in 1803 of Richard's daughter, Frances, to James Martin's son, John, and the young couple's move to Camden Place. Chislehurst.

Richard and Mary had a large family but only three of their offspring are buried here. George (1771-1821), the eldest son, married Mary Urry, his cousin, became a partner at the Grasshopper and bought Meyricks (now Bishop's Well), a substantial house on the Common and visible from the churchyard. Andrew (1787-1807) died aged 19 of typhus. He was the third son to bear his grandfather's name. It was clearly unlucky as the two other boys had died in infancy. Susanna (1783-1851) was one of three unmarried daughters to survive to adulthood. Henry too seems an unfortunate name. Their second son Henry (not buried here), spent some time in the Indian Civil Service before becoming a partner at the bank. His son, Henry St. George, aged six lies here, as does another grandson, Henry Martin, the 15- month old son of their daughter, Frances, and John Martin of Camden Place. Another grandchild who met a relatively early death was George's daughter, Elinor Hulse Berens. Her husband's family were the wealthy owners of Kevington Hall, St Mary Cray. Henry Hulse purchased Meyricks from his father-in-law but shortly after the couple moved in, Elinor died, leaving a two-year old daughter, also called Elinor. The remaining tomb-occupants – Emma, wife of Richard Norman and five- year old Marianne Stone, are two other granddaughters, the children of George and Mary, as was Mary who lived to 71.

In an age when continuance of the male line was vital for wealthy families, the Stones were remarkably unfortunate. Richard and Mary had 13 children of whom only two boys survived to adulthood. Henry had one son, who died in infancy, and three daughters. A second marriage produced three sons, all of whom died childless, and one daughter. George and his wife Mary had seven children, including just two sons, of whom only one, George (jun.), produced offspring - one daughter. With the death of her father in 1861 the Stone family became extinct in the male line and Coopers (see below) was sold to Mr Bowden.

10. Anne Taylor

Near the south porch is a cross in the ground to the left of the path leading from the lychgate

Miss Taylor joined the National School for Boys and Girls, now St Nicholas Church of England Primary School, in the mid-1850s as the Headmistress. Although the school was co-educational, the sexes were taught separately with a Master and Mistress responsible for each section, the Master having ultimate authority.

Unfortunately, Anne Taylor's time at the school does not appear to have been very happy or successful. Since its opening in 1836 the school had received at best only mediocre reports. A major problem was poor pupil attendance. In the school log book Miss Taylor regularly expresses her frustration at 'the difficulty of progressing favourably when so many children are absent day after day'. Parents were unused to putting their children's education before the demands of the household and the youngsters were sent out to gather wood or pick fruit as necessary. Other causes of absenteeism were sickness, distractions on the Common such as parties of day-trippers and troops of artillery from Woolwich undertaking exercises, and the weather. Anne Taylor believed Chislehurst children used inclement weather as an excuse for non-attendance: 'Bickley Park children seldom stay away for bad weather. Chislehurst children living close to the school are afraid to venture out.' Further stress was caused by members of the clergy and gentry who offered assistance with Religious Knowledge but whose own attendance was often unreliable. In 1865 a school inspector reporting on the girls' only moderate achievement acknowledged: 'The deficiency of the Mistress is not wholly responsible as a good deal of the instruction has been undertaken by the Ladies without any definite system.' Conditions at the school were unconducive to learning; the premises and furniture were sub-standard and sometimes it was so cold the children were unable to hold their writing implements. Miss Taylor was under pressure from parents and the Master. A father complained it was not worth paying two pence a week as his child had made no progress. She recorded another occasion when her authority was undermined: 'The Schoolmaster came in and boxed one girl's ears and pushed another down. Was that part of his duty? Resented this.' Eventually Miss Taylor had to leave on health grounds and died 14 months later on 23 April 1870.

Her relatively short life seems sad and unfulfilled. She came from a mining community in Gateshead. Her move to rural Chislehurst was a step up in the world but she lived alone at 2 Workhouse Place, part of the old Workhouse converted into tenements. She worked in difficult conditions and was frustrated by the children, their parents and some of the adults at the school. The inspectors were not impressed with her performance and in 1852 the Government introduced the notorious system of payment by results. She often took her pupils to see the weddings of local young ladies but died a spinster aged 45 after undergoing an operation in Guy's Hospital. The school was closed for her funeral so that the pupils could attend and the older girls processed behind the coffin. Her successor as Mistress was Martha Eggleton, who received a glowing report after her first year: 'The girls' school has improved considerably in her hands. The general tone seems to be rising. The standard of work is above that of any former years.'

Poor Miss Taylor.

11. Herbert Francis Murray

The grave with a cross and an anchor is located beside the south-east corner of the church.

In this spot are the graves of three members of the Murray family, the Rector's two wives and his young son, who all pre-deceased him.

Herbert Francis Murray was the younger son of the Rev. Canon Francis Murray, Rector of St Nicholas Church 1846-1902. Herbert's mother, Fanny, had died giving birth to him in 1850 and consequently his early death at sea at the age of twenty was especially poignant. The parish magazine recorded that he was: 'Born and brought up in the parish. There is a large circle of young persons to whom as playmate, companion or friend he had especially endeared himself and who, as we know, mourn his loss as that of a brother.'

On the night of 7 September 1870 sub-lieutenant Herbert Murray was aboard the frigate, HMS Captain, which having only recently completed sea trials, was cruising off Cape Finisterre with eleven other naval vessels. There had been controversy about the ship's new design - a warship powered by steam and sail with two rotating gun turrets. The Controller of the Navy, Ernest Reed, was especially concerned that the planned freeboard was only eight feet and due to a miscalculation was eventually just six feet. The designer was Capt. Cowper Phipps Coles, who finding himself in opposition to the Admiralty, had the ship built by Messrs. Laird of Birkenhead at his own expense. It was the only battleship to be privately designed and financed on behalf of the Navy.

Towards midnight a gale sprang up, the ship began to list and capsized with the loss of 480 lives, including Cowper Coles. There were only 27 survivors. A court martial following the disaster concluded that the ship was not stable and was built in opposition to the view of the Controller of the Navy.

The anchor on Herbert's gravestone is said to be a copy of HMS Captain's. At the top is inscribed: 'At midnight there was a cry made' (Matthew 25.6)

On the left-hand side are the lines from Psalm 77.19: 'Thy way is in the sea, and thy paths in the great waters and thy footsteps are not known.'

The marine imagery is continued on the right-hand side with the quotation from John Keble's poem from *The Christian Year* for the eighth Sunday after Trinity: 'Death only binds us to the bright shore of love.'

There are also a memorial window and brass plaque inside the church as well as a commemorative east window in the Church of the Annunciation in Chislehurst West. Other memorials to the dead are in St Paul's Cathedral, Westminster Abbey and in Portsmouth.

12. Noel H Paterson

This memorial stone is in the triangular plot opposite the west door of the church. Unfortunately the metal letters have been removed and the inscription is now difficult to read.

Noel Paterson's grave inscription states that he was killed, aged 33, by a sudden fall on the Lyskamm on 6 September 1877. The Lyskamm is the eighth highest mountain in the Swiss Alps with two summits separated by a ridge. The higher peak is the eastern summit at 4527m, nicknamed the Menschenfresser (Man Eater) due to the numerous accidents and fatalities. The ascent is not particularly difficult but dangerous, because of the snow cornices which hang along the 1000m ridge.

Noel Paterson was a young barrister, who with an M.A. from St John's College, Oxford, joined the Middle Temple in 1829. He lived with his aunt, Gracia Campbell and his three younger sisters at Achlion 8 Church Row and was an active member in the Parish. In his obituary he is remembered 'as an earnest and cheerful worker and a genial friend.

For many years he had identified himself with the management of the Village Hall and was always ready and willing to devote himself to any matter of parochial interest'.

Noel was a keen Alpinist and at 2am on the morning of September 6 he and his friend, William Lewis, a fellow barrister, together with three very experienced guides from the Knübel family, left the Riffel Hotel above Zermatt to ascend the Lykskamm (right). As they failed to return that evening, early the next day a party consisting of a Mr Carfraes and three guides set out to ascertain whether they had descended to the Italian side. Late that evening Mr Carfraes returned

with the sad news that the entire party had perished, having fallen some 1200 feet from a snow ledge on the Italian side of the mountain. Bad weather on Saturday prevented the large rescue party of 30 guides and porters from setting out. On Sunday the bodies were recovered and on Monday Noel Paterson and William Lewis were buried in the English churchyard, known as the Mountaineers' Graveyard, in Zermatt. The funeral was attended by visitors to the town, guests from the hotel and local inhabitants.

An account of the accident, which appeared in *The Spectator* on 15 September, made the point that: 'the bodies were found near the spot at which the accident to Mr Hayman and his party occurred last year. As the accident occurred from a well-known cause – the giving-way of a cornice or ledge of snow on the mountain-side – and as both of the unfortunate gentlemen were robust, experienced Alpine climbers, it is useless to draw from what has happened the usual moral of caution. The best eye will sometimes be deceived as to the bearing-capacity of snow, and guides and travellers alike must take their chance of such a disaster.'

In the parish of St Nicholas, Chislehurst a subscription was set up to raise money to help the widows of the three guides, their ten children and their 90-year-old mother. By coincidence all the families lived in the village of St Nicklaus near Zermatt.

13. George Somers Leigh Clarke

This grave is in the north section of the churchyard beside the right-hand edge of the path which leads from the east gate. It is a low tomb with a flat, floriated cross on top. The lettering is very weathered but his name is just decipherable.

Somers Leigh Clarke (1822-1882) was a well-regarded English architect, who lived in Chislehurst for many years. He was a pupil of Sir Charles Barry, architect of the Houses of Parliament and some of Clarke's work was incorporated in the final design for the 1849 rebuild.

He set up his own practice in Cockspur Street and on the basis of his association with Barry was invited to submit designs for some major London landmarks. Although unsuccessful in securing prestigious assignments such as the Law Courts and Midland Hotel at St Pancras, his drawings were acclaimed and his buildings were regularly illustrated in architectural magazines.

He designed both residential and civic buildings in London and the South East. There are many examples of his work in Chislehurst, the most important being in St Paul's Cray Road and Manor Park. The group of imposing red brick, tile-hung houses which abut St Paul's Cray Road have plaques with the date 1878 and their names – Crayfield, Cleeveland and Warren House. Further towards Royal Parade is The Old Rectory, a misleading name as it was in fact the Clergy House, commissioned by the Rector, Canon Murray. At the far end of Manor Park on the right is an impressive group of large houses, Harley, Pelham, Manor Place, Walsingham and Walpole, the latter designed by Somers Leigh Clarke for his own use.

In 1883 a coffee tavern, designed by Somers Leigh Clarke, opened at 43/45 Chislehurst High Street. It was a temperance establishment, which did not open on Sundays, and consequently did not survive long. The gable can just be seen over the shops which were built in front of it.

George Somers Leigh Clarke died at his home in 1882 and Walpole House has now been divided into five apartments.

A pen and ink drawing from The Builder

14. The Williams and Field Families

These adjacent graves are located on the right hand side of the path leading from Church Lane to Church Row. The Williams' tomb is low with a horizontal cross on top, that of Field has a broken cross.

The occupants of these adjacent graves were intimately linked. George Edward Field (not to be confused with the Chislehurst carriage proprietor of that name) was the son-in-law of William Williams and their families lived together. In the mid-nineteenth century Mr Williams leased from the Lord of the Manor a property on the Common, which he named Plas Gwyn, Welsh for White House, a pretty house which can be seen to the west of the churchyard across the Cockpit. In about 1870 he moved to Penrhos on Manor Park Road. Although he and his homes had Welsh names, William Williams was not born in Wales but at All Hallows in the City of London. He worked as a wharfinger, a riverside wharf proprietor, and George Field was a wharfinger's clerk. George, his wife Mary Anne and their two children, occupied the White House and Penrhos with William and his wife. There are three Mary Ann(e)s commemorated on the Williams' tombstone: Mary Ann Williams d. 1870, William's wife; Mary Anne Field d.1900, William's daughter and wife of George; and Mary Anne Field d. 1925, elder daughter of George and granddaughter of William. With them all living in the same household life must have been most confusing.

George Field was a very popular member of the community, a church warden, on the committee of the Literary Society and Honorary Secretary of the Village Hall. In Webb's *History of Chislehurst* he is described as 'Master of Revels to the parish for twenty-five years'. He organised village entertainments and was an accomplished actor and public speaker. The Prince Imperial attended a performance of Sheridan's *The Critic*, in which according to a reviewer, 'Mr Field played the double part of Lord Burleigh and the Beefeater with his accustomed talent'. Other members of the Dramatic Society must have felt their thespian activities very inadequate when faced with reviews such as the following from the Parish Magazine:

'Mr Baldwin was daring enough to read a piece, which has often been

29

recited by Mr Field, and it naturally fell flat .... The last piece by Mr Field was undoubtedly the best; he certainly is a long way in advance of the other amateur reciters.'

Success did not go to George's head. He was known to jump in at the last moment if an actor was indisposed and the appreciation of the community is illustrated by the fact that on his sudden death, aged 63, in 1893 they funded the erection of his tombstone, 'as a token of their esteem'.

15. Alexander and Elizabeth Gamble

Located in the north section of the graveyard, this gravestone is a polished granite cross on a two-tiered plinth.

The simple design and wording of this gravestone belie the exotic life which Alexander Gamble lived. He was a Scotsman from Ardrossan, whose father, John, was a farmer on the estate of the Earl of Eglinton. There is a suggestion that John Gamble was hung for horse-stealing and his 10-year-old son, a weaver, underwent equestrian training either in Scotland or France at the expense of a well-wisher. Whatever the truth, we do know that Alexander married Elizabeth Merry, the daughter of a stable-keeper from Leamington Spa, in 1841 and was next heard of in the service of Louis Napoleon, soon to become Napoleon III. He accompanied Napoleon at the coup d'état, and at the commencement of the Second Empire was given the position of Master of the Horse and equerry.

Life at the French Imperial court was one of over-indulgence and luxury. The extravagance extended to the stables where Gamble had charge of the largest stud in Europe; the Emperor kept 350 horses and 150 carriages. According to a contemporary account: 'The horse-boxes were in carved oak; the name of each animal might be read in a medallion at the head of its stall surmounted by an Imperial crown. Everything was on the grand scale: on the bitumous floor were modelled eaglets with outspread wings; the chains and garniture of the boxes and mangers were of brass and steel and shone like carbuncles.'

The huge riding-school contained a gently sloping staircase up and down which the horses sedately strutted and the centre of the grand hall was decorated with flowers and a fountain which 'discharged its waters through the jaws of two bronze dogs lying on marble pedestals'. In these opulent surroundings Gamble spent his days maintaining the horses in tip-top condition and entertaining the crowned heads of Europe, who included a tour of the renowned stables during their visits and bestowed many valuable gifts on him. He accompanied the Emperor into battle at Magenta, Solferino and Saarbrücken, where he acquitted himself well but was also present at the final disaster of Sedan. He witnessed

the interview between Bismark and Napoleon III and accompanied the Emperor into his internment at Wilhelmshöhe Palace, where his services were still required as Louis Napoleon was allowed to retain 22 horses. However, on the day after Empress Eugénie moved into Camden Place, her home in exile in Chislehurst on December 10 1870, the remainder of the horses, which had once belonged to the Emperor of the Second French Empire and been pampered in the stables of the Tuileries by Alexander Gamble, were sold at auction by 'a nobleman'.

When Napoleon was reunited with his family in Chislehurst, Gamble did not live with other members of the Imperial household but took lodgings in Church Row. Less than two years after his arrival in England, Napoleon III died. Gamble had accompanied him through triumph and defeat for nearly thirty years. In July 1879 Gamble attended a second Bonaparte funeral. The Prince Imperial had been killed in the Zulu wars and his body returned to Chislehurst for burial in St Mary's Catholic Church. In the funeral procession that made its slow way across the Common from Camden Place Gamble led the Prince's rider-less horse, Stag, immediately behind the gun carriage bearing the coffin. It was Gamble who had first taught the young Prince to ride and perform the stunt of mounting whilst the animal was in motion,

In 1880 Gamble, at 63, was approaching his own death which was reported widely: 'Alexander Gamble, the stud groom of the late Emperor Napoleon and a venerable and trusted follower of the Imperial dynasty, is lying seriously ill at Chislehurst, while little hope is entertained for his recovery. The ex-Empress has called several times recently to enquire after her old servant.' Elizabeth, Gamble's wife and a mere cipher in this story, is interred with him. She lived the 15 years of her widowhood with her niece, who ran a grocery store in Leamington Spa, a far cry from Paris and the Imperial court.

16. William Pett Ridge

The very plain and simple gravestone is located in the north section of the graveyard.

William Pett Ridge, born in Chartham, Kent in 1859, came from humble beginnings. His father was a railway porter and William worked as a railway clerk, whilst attending evening classes in further education at Birkbeck College in London. He began his literary career by contributing short stories to the *St James Gazette* and other magazines and became a prolific, best-selling author producing more than sixty works – novels, short stories, memoirs and plays. His first book was published in 1895 and his success was established in 1898 with the publication of *Mor'd Em'ly*, an amusing portrait of working-class life. His stories, which are sentimental, humorous, sympathetic to the underdog, and set in London, are clearly indebted to Dickens. In his hey-day Pett Ridge was extremely popular and recognised as a member of the Cockney School of writers, hence the gravestone inscription 'Friend of the Cockneys". He earned a very good living, four of his books were turned into silent films in the 1920s and he was a friend of H.G.Wells, another local writer. Although he is little remembered today, his work is still in print, but it seems very dated.

William also gave his time and money to good causes. He founded a babies' home in Hoxton in 1907 and was a visitor at Pentonville Prison.

Contemporaries said he was delightful and warm-hearted and was always ready to speak and write on behalf of good causes. He published a pamphlet calling for donations to purchase Petts Wood (no relation) in memory of William Willett, Chislehurst resident and proponent of Daylight Saving Time.

William appeared to be a confirmed bachelor but in 1909 he married Olga Hentsche and they had a son and daughter. He spent the last ten years of his life in Chislehurst, living first at Mead View, Green Lane and then at Ampthill, 3 Willow Grove Villas. He died in September 1930 aged 71. He was cremated at West Norwood and his ashes brought back to Chislehurst.

17. Jessie Drummond

The grave, marked by a small cross, is to be found in the north section of the churchyard beneath a large tree against the western fence.

Jessie Drummond was a Scotswoman, who at the age of 35 became the lady superintendent of St Michael's Orphanage, together with Maria Anderdon. Miss Anderdon, sister-in-law of Canon Murray, Rector of St Nicholas, had first opened the home with her sister in 1855 in a pair of cottages on St Paul's Cray Road. The occupants were two orphans and a dog. In 1861 they moved into part of the old workhouse on the Common. They could now accommodate 36 boys between the ages of four and twelve. With later extensions the number rose to 50.

Jessie was responsible for the day-to-day care and welfare of the boys, who attended the National School nearby. In their spare time they learned to net string bags, sew and embroider. Their handiwork was displayed and sold at the annual Open Day held on St Michael's Day, 29 September.

It was a notable occasion in the village social calendar. There was a full day of special events, which began with a service, conducted in the home's own chapel, by Canon Murray. Many old boys revisited on this day, testimony to the affection in which they held Jessie. As her gravestone inscription testifies: 'For 20 years she held with loving care the charge of the children of St Michael's Orphanage.' She died aged 54 on the Eve of St Michael's Day 1884 - a very happy coincidence.

The graves of the Anderdon sisters are nearby.

ST NICHOLAS CHURCH, CHISLEHURST

The church is first mentioned in a 1089 advowson from Bishop Gundulph of Rochester to the Cathedral Priory of St Andrew, but little of the Norman building remains.

In 1424 Thomas Walsingham purchased Scadbury Manor. The Scadbury Chapel and rood screen are attributed to his son, Thomas Walsingham II. An inscription on the Walsingham tomb refers to Thomas Walsingham IV, patron of Christopher Marlowe, playwright and Shakespeare's contemporary. On this flimsy basis in 1956 an American, Calvin Hoffman, in an attempt to establish the true authorship of Shakespeare's plays, gained permission to open the tomb. He found nothing.

The painted heraldic devices of Henry VI and Edward IV on the chapel south wall are possibly by William Camden, Clarenceux King-at-Arms and historian, who lived in Chislehurst between 1609 and 1623, and were perhaps commissioned to celebrate Walsingham's acquisition in 1611 of the Manor of Chislehurst.

On the newly-restored diamond-shaped hatchments are the coat of arms of the Townshends, later Lords of the Manor.

In Georgian times the church contained box pews and galleries for the musicians and singers. In 1849 these were removed when Canon Murray made major alterations and added the south aisle. This incorporated the original porch and those buried in or beside it, like Sir William Bowles, who in his will of 1680 expressed the wish to be buried 'in the church porch of Chislehurst Church ' close to his wife Margaret and brother Dr George Bowles. A tablet preserved from 1714 and now positioned above the south door reads: 'John Rands lies at the church door', which is clearly no longer true.

In 1857 a fire broke out in the bell chamber and sent the bells and spire crashing down. Fortunately, the speedy response of parishioners, who ferried 2,000 buckets of water from house-wells in Church Row, saved the rest of the church. Within a year all was restored.

A window funded by the congregation, featuring St Nicholas carrying a child, is dedicated to John Mitcham and William Steptoe, two choristers who died in the Great War. In 1920 the memorial chapel was dedicated to 51 parishioners killed in the War. After WWII 24 names were added.